CONOZCO LOS NÚMEROS
I KNOW NUMBERS

By Jon Welzen
Traducido por Fátima Rateb

Gareth Stevens
PUBLISHING

conceptos
básicos

Conozco los números.
¡Veo números!

I know numbers.
I see numbers!

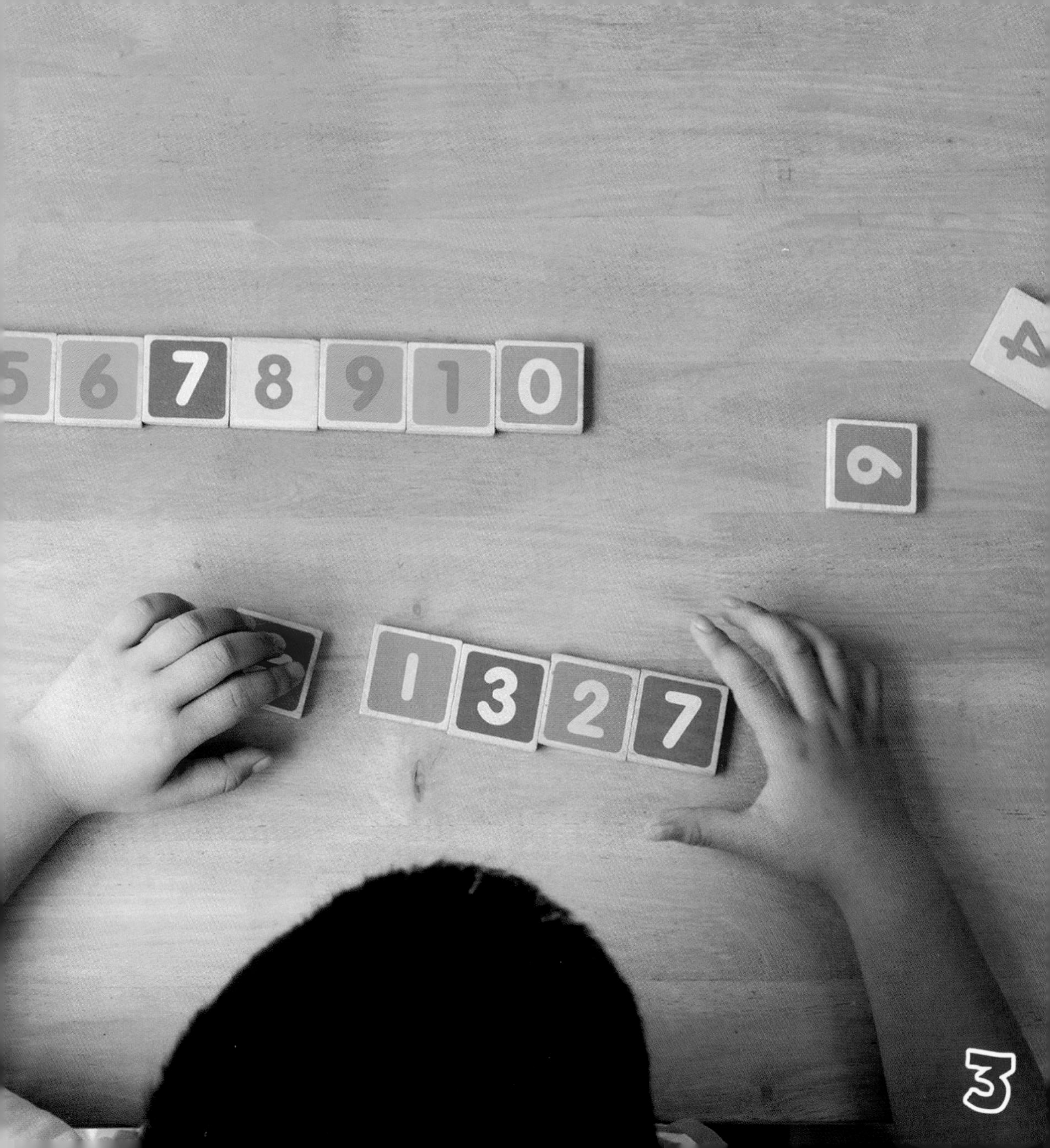
5 6 7 8 9 1 0
1 3 2 7

Veo 1 pastelito.

I see 1 cupcake.

Veo 2 manos.

I see 2 hands.

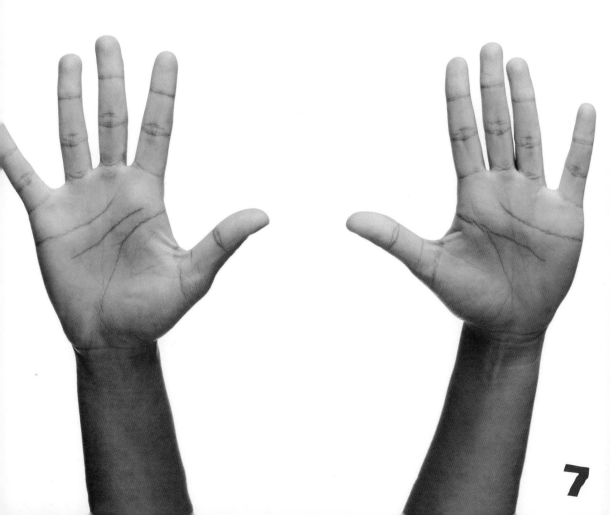

7

Veo 3 amigos.

I see 3 friends.

Veo 4 barquillos
de helado.

I see 4 ice cream cones.

11

Veo 5 bloques.

I see 5 blocks.

13

Veo 6 conejos.

I see 6 rabbits.

15

Veo 7 osos de peluche.

I see 7 teddy bears.

17

Veo 8 ranas.

- -

I see 8 frogs.

19

Veo 9 pelotas.

- -

I see 9 balls.

21

¡Veo 10 dedos del pie!
¿Qué números ves?

I see 10 toes!
What numbers
do you see?

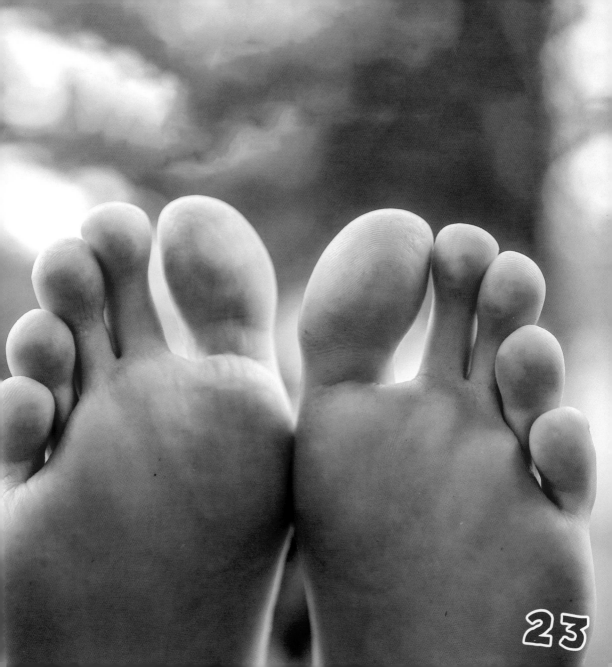

23

Please visit our website, www.garethstevens.com. For a free color catalog of all our high-quality books, call toll free 1-800-542-2595 or fax 1-877-542-2596.

Cataloging-in-Publication Data

Names: Welzen, Jon.
Title: I know numbers = Los números / Jon Welzen.
Description: New York : Gareth Stevens Publishing, 2017. | Series: What I know = Conozco los números | In English and Spanish
Identifiers: ISBN 9781482462036 (library bound)
Subjects: LCSH: Numbers, Natural–Juvenile literature. | Counting–Juvenile literature.
Classification: LCC QA141.3 W45 2017 | DDC 513.2–dc23

First Edition

Published in 2017 by
Gareth Stevens Publishing
111 East 14th Street, Suite 349
New York, NY 10003

Copyright © 2017 Gareth Stevens Publishing

Translator: Fátima Rateb
Editorial Director, Spanish: Nathalie Beullens-Maoui
Editor, English: Therese Shea
Designer: Sarah Liddell

Photo credits: Cover, p. 1 (stripes) Eky Studio/Shutterstock.com; cover, p. 1 (numbers) sxpnz/Shutterstock.com; p. 3 Kdonmuang/Shutterstock.com; p. 5 Billion Photos/Shutterstock.com; p. 7 Syda Productions/Shutterstock.com; p. 9 Robert Kneschke/Shutterstock.com; p. 11 szefei/Shutterstock.com; p. 13 Maryna Kulchytska/Shutterstock.com; p. 15 Dmitry Kalinovsky/Shutterstock.com; p. 17 (main) Fesus Robert/Shutterstock.com; p. 17 (left front bear) harmpeti/Shutterstock.com; p. 19 jacotakepics/Shutterstock.com; p. 21 Shi Yali/Shutterstock.com; p. 23 Annette Shaff/Shutterstock.com.

Printed in the United States of America

CPSIA compliance information: Batch #CW17GS: For further information contact Gareth Stevens, New York, New York at 1-800-542-2595.